DEMOS

First published in 2008

Magdalen House, 136 Tooley Street,
London, SE1 2TU, UK

ISBN 978-84180-194-0
Copy edited by Julie Pickard, London
Series design by modernactivity
Typeset by modernactivity
Printed by Lecturis, Eindhoven

Set in Gotham Rounded
and Baskerville 10
Cover paper: Arctic Volume
Text paper: Munken Print White

Acknowledgements

First, thanks go to AoC London for supporting this work. In particular, our thanks to Mila Caley, Vicki Fagg, Mark Hilton, Sue Parker and Sue Rimmer for their contributions to the project. Thank you also to the many people who played a part in the three workshops held at Demos, and to all those who participated in the research.

At Demos, thanks to all those who played a part in the project. Michael Janda provided research support, Alessandra Buonfino, Celia Hannon, William Higham and Simon Parker all offered feedback on drafts and Peter Harrington and Julie Pickard saw the pamphlet through production. From beyond Demos, thanks to Helen Casey, Judy Gawn and James Lee for their help.

And huge thanks go to Tom Jupp and Annette Zera, whose work, insights and support were invaluable.

Last, thanks to all those who took time out from learning English to share thoughts and experiences with us. We wish them all luck.

As ever, all errors and omissions remain our own.

Duncan O'Leary
April 2008

Contents

Acknowledgements 7

Executive summary 9

Introduction 17

1 Establishing the rationale for teaching English 23

2 ESOL policy changes and revisions 31

3 Future challenges for ESOL policy 37

4 More effective ways to reach those most in need 43

5 Personalising provision 53

Conclusions and recommendations 63

Afterword 71

Notes 77

References 85

Executive summary

About this report

This report explores which policies can encourage and support people to learn English in London. The research informing the report took place during a period of uncertainty and change for provision of English for Speakers of Other Languages (ESOL)[1] across the country. In that context, its purpose was to pinpoint the value of English language provision for individuals, communities and London's economy – and to find strategies that reflect and fulfil that promise. Based on six months of research, the report identifies where existing policy needs to be reviewed, developed or supplemented to meet the needs of London and its people. Although the report focuses on the challenge of London, it has implications for national policy. The research process involved:

- interviews with more than 40 learners enrolled on ESOL courses in London
- a discussion group with people not accessing ESOL courses
- three expert workshops, involving academics, college representatives, community groups and government agencies
- a desk-based review of the literature and evidence on English language policy

Our argument

The value of English – and the policy challenge

The English language is a vital part of London's future. The ability to speak English empowers people to take control of their everyday lives; it enables people to find employment and achieve progression in work; it helps people communicate and interact with one another in communities; and it supports parents to boost their children's life chances. These four areas amount to a compelling rationale to make English language learning a priority for policy in London and across the UK.

However, recent estimates suggest there are around 600,000 people of working age in London who have varying levels of need for English language learning.[2] And, following a period in which national spending on ESOL tripled over three years,[3] there are finite public resources available.

These three factors – the importance of the English language to London; the level of need in the capital; and the reality of finite resources – combine to create a policy challenge. Policy makers must find ways to make courses accessible to people from all backgrounds and responsive to the needs of each individual. This report deals with that challenge on two levels: by looking at, first, how entitlements are constructed and, second, how policy shapes the delivery of courses in practice.

Funding ESOL

Where funding is concerned, our core argument is that entitlements should follow the same set of principles as literacy and numeracy provision, without necessarily having the same set of specific arrangements. Put simply, some ESOL learners enjoy relatively high spending power, in a way that is not the case for other literacy and numeracy client groups. It is possible to require English lessons but enjoy high earning power in the labour market.

The principle of a means test, of some description, is the right way of focusing limited resources on the most disadvantaged: those people who cannot afford to pay for themselves. However, the nature of the means test needs to be reviewed to achieve its goals in practice. Our research suggests that the current set of arrangements are too inflexible and risk failing to reach some of the most vulnerable and disengaged learners. This is especially the case for spouses who may have no access to family finances or personal spending power. To address this, entitlements should treat people as individuals rather than as members of families; they should be structured around non-employment rather than unemployment.

Furthermore, research visits to colleges and interviews with ESOL learners make it clear that funding systems need to be able to distinguish between learners with low levels of prior education and those who are already literate and numerate in their own language. People who are learning basic literacy and numeracy through a foreign language are likely to require longer, more intensive courses than those who can already read and write in their own language. This is already reflected in the best practice of many providers, but needs to be reflected in policy to ensure a systematic approach. Learners with very little prior education should be afforded more funding as a result. A holistic needs assessment to establish levels of funding for each individual would be the best way of achieving this.

Finally, the effects of targets need to be reviewed to ensure protection for entry-level courses, which are important stepping stones to progression. The government should introduce a measure for entry-level courses if necessary.

Delivering ESOL

Where delivery is concerned, discussions with ESOL learners and other ESOL stakeholders reveal that the system makes too many assumptions about what people are looking for and need from a course. Qualifications need to become more flexible, along the lines of the proposed credit system, and there should be experimentation with different forms of assessment such as practitioner assessment for a certain number of credits of learning within each qualification. This flexibility would help personalise courses and contribute to bridging the gap between the education and employment systems. Courses and qualifications need to provide progression, but they also need to be fitted around learners, rather than vice versa.

We also argue that policy could do more to support learning and active participation outside the classroom. For example, learners could be pointed towards opportunities to practise their English through options like mentoring, volunteering or work-shadowing opportunities. We conclude with some lessons for future policy and strategy.

Our recommendations

Many of the issues discussed in this report are being addressed through good practice in colleges and other providers. However, the issue is whether policy builds on these approaches and supports taking them to scale. The report and recommendations focus on the role that policy can play in shaping the whole system. The recommendations are therefore directed at the government, the Learning and Skills Council (LSC), the London Skills and Employment Board (LSEB) and the Mayor of London.

Funding and entitlements

Recommendation 1: To ensure that spouses are not excluded unintentionally from provision, entitlements should treat people as individuals rather than as members of families – they should be structured around *non-employment* rather than unemployment.

Recommendation 2: To build flexibility, or personalisation, into the system, all entitlements should be established through a personal needs assessment, which would take account, among other factors, of prior levels of education in their own language.

Recommendation 3: During the needs assessment, people should be given advice about entitlements, assistance in finding the right course, guidance about how best to accredit existing skills, and direction towards immersion opportunities to supplement their learning in the classroom.

Recommendation 4: On grounds of humanitarianism and social cohesion, funding arrangements for refugees and asylum seekers should also be reviewed. Entitlements should be activated after eight weeks, the time by which the majority of initial asylum decisions have to have been taken.

Recommendation 5: To reflect social goals the government should aim not just to meet demand, but to meet *need* by connecting with the hardest to reach. This would involve outreach work, partnership with the third sector in signposting opportunities and guidance for other local public services.

Recommendation 6: These recommendations have cost implications. Where feasible, extra funding to make these changes should come from across government, reflecting the full range of goals associated with ESOL learning – personal empowerment, enhanced employability, improved social cohesion and greater intergenerational mobility. To ensure coherence, one department should take the lead on ESOL policy and funding control.

Delivery

Recommendation 7: To create options for learning that meet people's specific needs, the government should establish a credit framework for ESOL courses, to provide both the option of shorter courses and a platform for progression.

Recommendation 8: To add flexibility to the system, national policy should experiment with different forms of assessment – such as practitioner assessment for a certain number of credits of learning within each qualification – and ensure that embedded ESOL courses are eligible for fee remission.

Recommendation 9: To bring the learner's voice to the heart of the system there should be a national online system of feedback, through which learners would reflect on their experience of a course on its completion.

Recommendation 10: To protect entry-level courses, which are important stepping stones to progression, the effects of targets need to be reviewed. Targets need to be understood as approximate measures of progress, not outcomes in themselves, if policy is to avoid unintended consequences. More tangibly, the government should introduce a measure for entry-level courses if they are going to prove hard to fund otherwise.

Future policy and strategy

Recommendation 11: To ensure openness and transparency in future policy, the Mayor of London and the government should set out a clear statement of goals for English language policy in London.

Recommendation 12: To support effective policy and proper accountability, the government should commit to formal evaluations of English language policy against its stated objectives.

Introduction

London in 2008 stands as a global city in almost every sense. Financially, it has become a world leader, overtaking New York as a global centre for commerce and finance.[4] Culturally, it has reached a level of diversity not matched by any other city in the world, with 350 languages spoken by residents of the city.[5] Communication links with the rest of the world proliferate: there are more international phone calls made from London than from any other place in the world.[6]

An important driver of this cultural and economic dynamism is migration: 2001 census figures identify 1.9 million people born outside the UK living in London.[7] As with the UK as a whole, net migration into London has been rising steadily in recent years, with emigration remaining relatively steady, in contrast to rising numbers of people entering the capital (see figure 1).[8]

This growth in inward migration is, in large part, a reflection of the fact that traditionally new migrants to the UK have been most likely to settle in urban areas – and in London in particular.[9]

The natural result of this is that large numbers of people living in Britain's capital speak English as their second language, with many lacking basic fluency in English. In London, there are an estimated 600,000 people of working age who have varying levels of need for English language learning.[10] London therefore finds itself in a unique position, delivering half the ESOL provision in the whole of the UK as a result.[11]

Figure 1 **International migration into and out of London ('000s)**

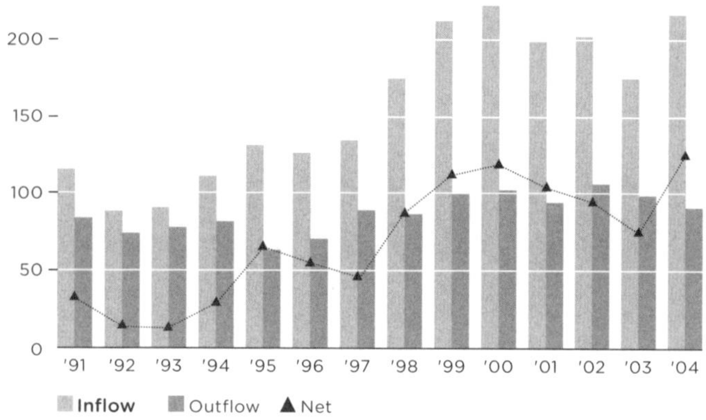

Source: ONS Regional Trends 39
Note: National Health Service Central Register and International Passenger Survey.

Aims of this report

This report sets itself the goal of contributing towards policy – set by the government, the Learning and Skills Council (LSC), the London Skills and Employment Board (LSEB) and the Mayor of London – which will ensure that all Londoners can speak English. As such, it is targeted at policy makers in those institutions, although we hope it will prove of use to English language practitioners and others with a stake in the issues that we discuss.

The reasons we identify for the importance of learning English fall under four main categories:

- *Empowerment*: Speaking English plays an important part in helping people take control of their lives.
- *Economics and employability*: There is evidence that suggests that speaking English is an important building block of employability. It helps people progress in education and find work, to their benefit and to the benefit of London as a whole.

- *Integration and social cohesion*: Speaking English helps people communicate with one another and is particularly important as London becomes more diverse.
- *Intergenerational social mobility*: Speaking English helps parents contribute as fully as possible to their children's development and educational attainment.

We then go on to outline the changes needed to the organisation of provision and its funding to reflect these aims.

Structure of this report

The report starts by examining the impact of speaking English – the value to individuals, to the British economy, to London's communities and economy, and for future generations. The remainder of the report is dedicated to exploring which policies can help to encourage and support English learning in the capital. This discussion begins by examining the current policy position, including recent changes to funding and eligibility for subsidised ESOL courses. It then explores some of the shortfalls of the current approach, before concluding with recommendations for change.

The report and recommendations are based on six months of research involving:

- interviews with more than 40 learners enrolled on ESOL courses in London
- a discussion group with people not accessing ESOL courses
- three expert workshops, involving academics, college representatives, community groups and government agencies
- a desk-based review of the literature and evidence on English language policy

Our argument

The report is centred around the following core arguments:

- Learning English is a distinct form of learning from literacy and numeracy.

- Entitlements, funding and delivery arrangements for English language learning should follow the same set of *principles* as other 'Skills for Life' provision (ie should be focused on those most in need and tailored to each individual).
- However, the diversity of English language learners means that *arrangements* for English language learning may not be exactly the same as other areas of learning that fall under the Skills for Life banner.
- Put simply, some ESOL learners have relatively high spending power, in a way that is not the case for other Skills for Life client groups. The principle of a means test of some description is the right way of focusing limited resources on the most disadvantaged.
- Though the principles of a means test may be sound, some radical changes are needed to the way entitlements are put together to meet the needs of the most vulnerable learners in practice.
- The current set of policies and funding arrangements risks unintended consequences, preventing as many people from learning English as possible – with negative consequences for individuals, communities, the economy and future generations.
- The objective of a 'demand-led' system is mistaken: the priority for government is to meet *need*, rather than simply to meet the demand of those who register for English language learning.
- Significant changes should be made to funding and delivery arrangements to help meet that need.
- These include new ways of connecting with *potential* learners; a system of entitlements more sensitive to people's personal needs and circumstances; more flexibility about which courses of learning can be funded; and a more strategic approach binding together the efforts of different government departments and agencies.

1 Establishing the rationale for teaching English

The English language sits at the heart of a number of heated – and crowded – debates. Questions around economic success, social inclusion, integration, citizenship and national identity all affect, and *are affected by,* the availability, take-up and quality of ESOL provision.

Perhaps as a result of the number of issues, interest groups and organisations involved in these overlapping debates, questions around learning English are laden with complexity. The risk is that policy reflects a partial view of the issues (such as short-term cost concerns affecting one government department), rather than a cross-cutting analysis of why learning English matters – and how policy should reflect that.

This chapter identifies four core reasons, or broad headings, to explain why learning English matters to London and why ESOL courses, from entry level through to level 2, are so important. The four headings discussed below emerged from interviews with ESOL learners themselves, from the evidence we already have on the value of speaking English and from workshops with ESOL stakeholders. These serve as the basis for the analysis in the remainder of the report. They provide a rationale that could be extrapolated beyond London and against which success or failure of policy could be tested in the future. Our four reasons are:

- everyday empowerment
- economics and employability
- integration and social cohesion
- intergenerational social mobility

Everyday empowerment

ESOL learners were clear in the interviews conducted for this report that the biggest difference that learning English had made to their lives was that they felt a much greater degree of control over their everyday experiences. Many described difficulties that they had faced over a number of years with tasks such as making appointments at doctors' surgeries, dealing with officials and official correspondence, booking plumbers or even communicating with people serving them in shops. Through the courses that they had enrolled on many of these barriers were now being removed – leaving them happier and more in control of their lives.

This change that ESOL learners observed in their lives underlines an important political point: empowering people should be a moral goal for government. Modern societies are characterised by inequalities not just in wealth, but also in power: the ability for people to map out their own futures and play an active part in the world around them. As Demos has argued before: 'The goal of democracy is self-government. This is the root of the ancient democratic ideal, but it has been lost from the twentieth century western models of politics.'[12] Low fluency in the language of a society amounts to powerlessness in everyday life. It creates barriers to even the most routine of activities, let alone to playing an active part in civic life. Policies that support people to learn English should therefore be inescapably part of any political agenda with designs on putting people in control of their own lives – something espoused by politicians across the political divide.[13] English language is about positive freedom: the freedom for people to go about their lives and to play a part in their communities.

Economics and employability

London not only has a lower employment rate than the rest of the country,[14] but there is a striking correlation between the ability to speak English and the likelihood of being in work.[15] Employment is of course a complex issue, but the evidence indicates that proficiency in English relates strongly to employability (see figure 2). Qualitative evidence from our research also reflects this; many of the learners who were interviewed for this project had enrolled to equip themselves with language skills for vocational learning or direct employment.

Figure 2 **Employment rates by qualifications level and first language, Greater London, 2003 (%)**

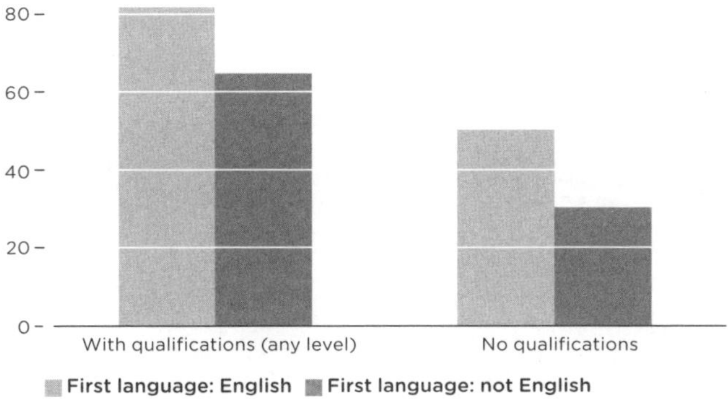

Source: *Labour Force Survey* (Jun–Aug 2003)
Note: Employment rate (%), persons of working age excluding full-time students.

A fluent population, of course, also has value to London as a whole – it is likely to mean more people finding paid employment and contributing to the city's economy. To add urgency to this, the migrant population has a younger age structure than the existing population in the UK, meaning that migrants are more likely to be of working age than the rest of the population. As a group, migrants now comprise one-third of London's working-age population.[16]

Moreover, it is also clear that this is not just an issue about non-employment (people choosing not to work). Research commissioned by the mayor has found that 'the *unemployment* (people in the labour market, but out of work) rate for Londoners with English as a second language is 14 per cent, twice as high as the rate for those with English as a first language'.[17] Around one in five people with English as another language have reported lack of English skills as an impediment to finding or keeping employment.[18] In other words, there can be significant economic consequences associated with fluency in English. Individuals are likely to benefit for themselves, through increased employability, and the rest of London is more likely to reap the benefits of the contribution that migrants have to offer.

Integration and social cohesion

London benefits hugely from its cultural and ethnic diversity, as a recent survey commissioned by the mayor's office found: 'London's cultural diversity is enjoyed by 83 per cent of people in the capital and 69 per cent believe there are good relations between different racial, ethnic and religious communities.'[19] Londoners clearly feel that the capital is a better place because of migration.

But the nature of modern communities – their fluidity, their frequent lack of shared history, their unfamiliarity – can also create challenges. One long-standing concern is of ethnic segregation. The Cantle report, commissioned after the race riots in Bradford in 2001, described a 'depth of polarisation' with communities living 'a series of parallel lives'.[20] The evidence suggests that the same can also be true in the labour market. As the government's Equalities Review pointed out, those from minority ethnic groups remain more likely to be concentrated in a smaller number of sectors, in junior positions, and in low-paid jobs.[21]

And to add to these more traditional concerns, the American sociologist Robert Putnam has pointed towards a link between cultural diversity and trust, arguing that:

In the long run immigration and diversity are likely to have important cultural, economic, fiscal, and developmental benefits. In the short run, however, immigration and ethnic diversity tend to reduce social solidarity and social capital. New evidence from the US suggests that in ethnically diverse neighbourhoods residents of all races tend to 'hunker down'. Trust (even of one's own race) is lower, altruism and community cooperation rarer, friends fewer.[22]

In interviews for this project, many ESOL learners felt a sense of duty to play their part in social integration – and expressed concern that before they had enrolled on courses they had been unable to communicate effectively with others in their neighbourhood. Typically, governments struggle to respond to these kinds of challenges. Positive relations within and between communities cannot easily be 'delivered' in the same way as a new hospital or library might be. Social integration and cohesion depend on many factors, often intangible, that can be difficult to address directly through the law.

The evidence does suggest, however, that language can be an important positive contributor to these goals. An audit of the evidence in community cohesion conducted by the government found, for example, that:

Inability to speak English has been highlighted... as a critical barrier to integration and communication for new arrivals. We are also conscious that lack of language skills in settled communities can create social distance... as well as being linked to social isolation, they highlight that lack of common language means residents lack a key tool for building trust.[23]

Similarly, the independent Commission for Integration and Cohesion found that speaking English is 'fundamental to integration and cohesion – for settled communities, new communities, and future generations of immigrants'.[24] In a policy area with few of the traditional 'levers' available to government, helping people to learn English looks like one of the few clear-cut things that governments can rely on to help communities enjoy living together.

Intergenerational social mobility

Another core goal for government – accepted across the political spectrum – is to improve the life chances of future generations. As we learn more about the determinants of social mobility, the ability of parents to speak English – allowing them to help their children learn to read and write and to interact with children's services – becomes clearer. Stakeholders who attended workshops held during the research echoed the views of ESOL learners themselves about the importance of being able to understand what their children were learning and to communicate with teachers in schools.

English language provision, therefore, needs to be understood as part of a wider battle to improve the life chances of future generations. While social mobility is regarded as a political priority, it has not improved over the last 30 years.[25] While the proportion of those from the poorest fifth of families gaining a degree has risen from 6 per cent to 9 per cent, the equivalent rates for the richest fifth have risen from 20 per cent to 47 per cent. When compared with other nations, Britain lags behind Canada, Denmark, Finland, Germany, Norway and Sweden where social mobility is concerned.[26]

As more evidence emerges, it becomes clearer that the early years of a child's life are vital in setting a platform for outcomes later on. Indeed the government's own research indicates how early social circumstances can affect outcomes, finding that 'by the age of six, the low-IQ child from the rich family has already overtaken the poor but clever child'.[27]

One of the important determinants of *successful* outcomes emerges as parenting.[28] Charles Desforges, of the University of Exeter, has shown that parenting has four times more impact than schooling on the educational outcomes for primary school age children – and that parenting accounts for a quarter of the attainment of top-scoring children at the age of 16.[29] Further research for the Effectiveness of Pre-school and Primary Education (EPPE) project has found that 'a parent who reads with their child, helps them to play with letters, learn songs or rhymes, paint, draw or visit the library, is providing a strong Home Learning Environment (HLE) for their child'.[30]

However, set against this growing body of evidence is the statistic that around one-quarter of all London's parents have English as a second language.[31] This, of course, does not mean that speakers of other languages will not be able to bring their children up successfully and support their development. But interaction with children's services, let alone reading to a child in the evening, are all likely to be easier and more fruitful if parents are confident and capable of speaking English. Supporting more parents to learn English represents one way of addressing the fact that pupils from some ethnic backgrounds are born less likely to leave school with qualifications that those with the same socio-economic status.[32]

These four areas amount to a compelling rationale to make English language learning a priority for policy in London and across the UK and underline the value of the ESOL courses being funded and delivered across the capital. They should also serve as criteria with which to judge the success of policy. In the following chapter we look at the policy trajectory for English language learning, tracking some significant changes to the way provision is funded and delivered.

2 ESOL policy changes and revisions

This report, of course, is not the first to identify the importance of language to social and economic success in London and the UK more widely. Teaching English to speakers of other languages has been a feature of public policy for several decades already. In recent years, however, governments have faced dual pressures: first, the imperative to help the working-age population attain higher skills; second, sharp rises in the number of migrants entering the country without English as a first language. This chapter explores:

- the perceived tension between the literacy and numeracy goals of the Skills for Life strategy and the rise in demand for ESOL provision
- the revisions to policy first proposed by the government to deal with this tension
- the concerns raised following those proposals and the subsequent adjustments to policy

The publication of the Leitch Review of Skills in 2006 highlighted the growing social and economic importance of the first of these two issues. The review highlighted two startling facts: that 70 per cent of the 2020 working-age population has already left full-time education, and that there are approximately five million adults in the UK without the literacy levels expected of an 11-year-old.[33] This challenge is mirrored in London, with the latest *Labour Force Survey* showing that over 600,000 adults in London have no qualifications.[34] Qualifications, of course, are not the same as skills, but these figures give an indication of the challenge where adult learning is concerned in London. These statistics lie behind the urgency to attract more adults back into education, particularly at a time in which the proportion of low-skilled jobs available in London is set to fall over the coming years.

Basic skills, therefore, are rightly a political priority, reflecting not just the economic challenges and opportunities of globalisation, but a moral commitment to helping people from all backgrounds fulfil their potential. Running alongide this drive to upskill the existing population, however, has been the growing number of migrants entering the country without fluency in English. In particular, the entry of new states into the EU following the Treaty of Accession 2003 – and the decision of the government not to enforce transitional controls on migration from those countries thereafter – has led to rising demand for English language learning.

From 2001 to 2006 ESOL enrolments rose nationally from 158,000 to 538,000, causing spending on ESOL to triple in the space of five years.[35] In London, this meant a situation in which ESOL provision came to account for nearly two-thirds of all Skills for Life provision, with public investment in ESOL reaching £180 million annually.[36]

This rise in demand for – and spending on – ESOL led to concerns on two levels. First, that funding was not being targeted effectively at those with the greatest need.[37] And second, that spending on ESOL was diverting money away from other basic skills provision and priorities.[38]

Changes to entitlements

The result of these concerns was a set of proposals to change funding criteria for ESOL provision. The proposals, introduced by the LSC, meant that: 'From 2007/08, ESOL learning will no longer attract automatic fee remission. Free tuition will only be available to priority groups – primarily people who are unemployed or receiving income based benefits.'[39] These initial changes are described in more detail below.

A description of the original proposals for change is followed by detail of further revisions that were made to policy before its implementation. These secondary changes were a response to a Race Equality Impact Assessment (REIA) on policy proposals, and wider concerns expressed by the Mayor of London, refugee lobby groups and ESOL teaching professionals. The initial proposed changes were:

- Automatic fee remission for ESOL courses undertaken by British citizens and permanent residents has been removed. Those receiving unemployment benefits and other forms of income-based government benefit (ie tax credits) will still be entitled to full fee remission,[40] while other ESOL students will pay between 19 per cent and 37.5 per cent of their course costs.[41]
- Employers who bring in migrants for work will be expected to share the costs of provision. For instance, in the new 'ESOL for work' qualifications, the employer or the individual employee pays £330 out of an £880 course cost, while the government funds the remainder.[42] This was a softening of the LSC's initial position that 'employers who have recruited workers from outside the UK [will be expected] to bear the full cost of any necessary English-language training'.[43]
- Asylum seekers aged 16–18 and those aged 19 or older who had been granted refugee status, humanitarian protection or discretionary leave to remain would be eligible for full ESOL fee remission.[44] All other asylum seekers would be ineligible, as they are not eligible for the government benefits outlined above that attract full fee remission.

Concerns and revisions to policy

These proposed changes were met with concerns of adverse impacts on English language learning. Among the most unpopular changes was the removal of full fee remission for asylum seekers aged 19 or older until they had been granted refugee status, humanitarian protection or discretionary leave to remain – a process that generally takes several months, and sometimes much longer.[45] This led the government to announce some modifications to the initial proposals outlined below, which also responded to complaints raised in the REIA. There were also further complaints about potentially discriminatory differences between the new ESOL entitlements scheme and arrangements for literacy and numeracy training provision. These are discussed later. Specific revisions to policy have been as follows:

- reinstating eligibility for further education for asylum seekers without a decision after six months – six months is the Public Service Agreement target for asylum seeker procession, by which time at least 90 per cent of asylum seekers should have a decision
- reinstating eligibility for asylum seekers unable to leave the country for reasons beyond their control
- providing an additional £4.6 million in 2007/08 Learner Support Hardship Funds to support vulnerable learners, including spouses and low-paid workers – intended to assist those who may not qualify for full fee remission, due to their spouse working for instance, but who are unable to afford fees
- accepting a wider range of documentation to determine eligibility in recognition that people in need of ESOL may not yet have sufficient English skills to fill out more complex forms[46]

While these concessions were welcomed by refugee advocates and ESOL professionals, the general consensus among these groups was that they did not go far enough to alleviate ESOL access difficulties for disadvantaged groups caused by the new eligibility requirements. Many thought that the £4.6 million in Learner Support Hardship Funds would fail adequately to compensate for fee payments. The six-month gap between asylum seeker arrival and eligibility for ESOL provision was also heavily criticised, with James Lee from the British Refugee Council describing it as: 'six months of exclusion not just from FE [further education], but from the labour market, which will require additional investment later on'.[47]

These continuing criticisms led the mayor of London and the LSEB to negotiate a one-year transition funding package for ESOL provision in London, on the basis that there would be substantial reform to provision, including a stronger focus on employability. The package involved an extra £5 million contributed by the London Development Agency matched by £10 million extra from the LSC. This was intended to offset potential £1 million funding losses for nine of London's leading ESOL providers. However, as a one-off payment, it seems unlikely that it will contribute to the long-term future of ESOL provision in the capital.[48]

Finally, in January 2008, the Secretary of State for Innovation, Universities and Skills announced a new consultation, expressing the aim that 'ESOL funding should be more specifically targeted to foster community cohesion and integration in our communities'.[49] This document sets out the following indicative priorities:

- legal residents who might reasonably be expected to be in the country for the foreseeable future
- excluded women or those who are at risk of being excluded, particularly those who are parents with children under 16 years
- parents or carers within families at risk of multiple or complex problems
- those having no or low levels of literacy in their own language
- those who have not had any secondary education
- refugees and asylum seekers who are still in the country beyond six months awaiting a decision on their status or cannot return home

These issues – and the wider debate that has surrounded changes to ESOL policy – are discussed in the following chapters.

3 Future challenges for ESOL policy

An important feature of the changes described in the last chapter is that entitlements for learning English now differ from other Skills for Life entitlements. Where ESOL entitlements are constructed according to financial position, other Skills for Life entitlements are based on levels of prior achievement. This chapter argues the following:

- The government should clarify the rationale behind the different funding arrangements to avoid the potential for misunderstanding of policy.
- Literacy and numeracy needs can serve as a proxy for a means test for English speakers, given the correlation between low levels of literacy and numeracy and unemployment.
- By contrast, migrants are a far less homogenous group, with some enjoying high earning power and others significantly less well educated and well off.
- The diversity of ESOL learners means that arrangements for English language learning cannot be *exactly the same* as other Skills for Life arrangements if they are to follow the broader principle of being focused on those in most need.
- While the principle of treating English language learning differently may make sense, there need to be revisions to current policy for it to achieve its goals.

The National Institute of Adult Continuing Education (NIACE) among others has raised the possibility that current policy may be discriminatory, arguing that:

It would be unacceptable to remove that [universal] entitlement from ESOL learners while retaining it for literacy and numeracy. Such a course of action would be unfair and discriminatory. For the same reasons it would not be right to introduce a means-tested regime for ESOL learners alone.[50]

Similarly, others have argued that the decision to restrict funding because there is *too much demand* runs counter to the direction of skills policy more generally towards a demand-led system.[51] The position of the LSC is that:

Given the scale of demand and the pressure on resources, we must focus public investment on provision for those most at risk of disadvantage; and we should not support large-scale demand from those who can pay for their language learning. This is in line with the government's strategy for rebalancing costs of adult learning, and the principle that public funding should be directed towards those with the greatest need for support.[52]

It is important that the government and the mayor are able to clarify their positions on this. The most likely, reasonable and coherent explanation for the different structure of entitlements is that a level 2 Skills for Life entitlement for literacy and/or numeracy learners is *effectively* a means test, given the clear correlation between qualification levels and employment outcomes (see figure 3). The evidence shows that:

- Over half of those people in London with no qualifications are out of work (56 per cent).[53]
- Those in work with low or no qualifications are paid significantly less than those qualified to the equivalent of two A-levels or higher.[54]
- Londoners in work with low, or no, qualifications are also less likely to benefit from training than their more qualified peers, limiting their opportunities for progression.[55]

In other words, literacy and numeracy qualifications can be used as a proxy for a means test because we know that they are a reliable way of focusing publicly funded provision on those most in need.

Figure 3 **Employment rates in London by qualification level, 2005 (%)**

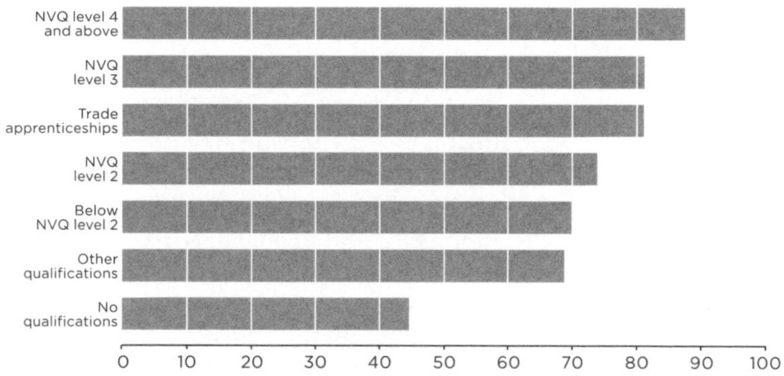

Source: Annual Population Survey, 2005

The situation with migrants, in contrast, is more complex. Data compiled by the LSEB shows that the earnings of migrant workers are relatively polarised: they are a far less homogenous group than those people fluent in English but with low or no qualifications. The LSEB data shows that:

Within the migrant population there is considerable polarity in earnings. Workers from high income countries earn relatively high [hourly] pay rates (£14.29) – 42 per cent more than the rates for workers from developing country groups (£10.05) and 11 per cent higher than rates for UK-born Londoners (£12.91).[56]

Similarly, data from the last census shows the vast differences in outcomes experienced by migrants from different parts of the world. Over half of all Somalis in London find themselves unemployed, for example, while unemployment rates for migrant groups from Germany, India, Italy and Kenya are all below the London average of just over 7 per cent.[57]

This is, in no small part, a reflection of the different qualification levels that people arrive in the country with.

Migrants with qualifications are twice as likely to be in employment as those with no qualifications. And when the evidence is examined closely, again it becomes clear that there are huge disparities between groups. Two-thirds of migrants from Argentina, Korea or Russia have high-level qualifications, for example, compared with just 15 per cent of Somalis.[58] Research visits to colleges during this project reinforce the point: displaced graduates and doctors from Afganistan enrol for ESOL courses alongside refugees from much poorer countries from around the world, where education systems are far less established and people have had far fewer opportunities – if any – to learn and progress.

The key point, then, is that while a significant proportion of migrants enter the country with high earning power, others most certainly do not. And unlike the very clear pattern where qualifications are concerned for English speakers, there are huge differences in outcomes between different migrant groups. Those qualified only to low levels are likely to be paid poorly – if they defy the odds to find work – and have comparatively fewer opportunities to progress.

In other words, different approaches should be adopted for those most in need and those who can afford to make their own contribution – not on the basis of where people were born. It would be wrong to treat migrants differently within the welfare state *simply because they are migrants*. But a policy based on helping those most in need can still recognise that the needs of migrants can differ radically from one individual to another. To take an extreme case, a wealthy entrepeneur moving to the country should be expected to pay for their own English classes, while someone drawing benefits should not.

Some employed migrants are relatively wealthy and can afford to make their own contributions while others need significant financial support from the state. Some of our interviewees had expected to pay for their course and were able to do so, while others were clear that they would never have been able to enrol without financial help. The potential for these disparities is not nearly so strong with other basic skills areas such as literacy and numeracy, where those without these skills are unlikely to be in work and highly unlikely to be in well-paid work.

However, while the principle of treating English language learning differently, and applying a means test on that basis may make sense, this does not mean that the way in which those principles have been implemented is effective or sustainable as things stand. The changes may have been made with good intentions, but, as we argue in the following chapter, they require further adaptation to achieve their goals.

4 More effective ways to reach those most in need

The core principle behind the changes to ESOL funding was to ensure that 'public funding should be directed towards those with the greatest need for support'.[59] Important questions remain as to whether this is being achieved in practice in London and more widely in the UK. This chapter argues that:

- Current policy may adversely affect, in various ways, some groups most in need, including spouses, asylum seekers and those on the threshold of the means test.
- Policy is not sufficiently sensitive to help meet the needs of English learners with radically different starting points and educational backgrounds.

To a certain degree, the impact of the changes to policy is difficult to untangle at this early stage. The extra funding made available in London by the LSC and the mayor, while important and welcome for this year, makes this process difficult by masking the impact of the changes to funding. Similarly, a number of colleges and other providers have chosen to cross-subsidise ESOL provision with money gained from other sources, muddying the water still further. The real impact of changes will be unclear until a full evaluation is conducted.

What this report can do is point to areas that need to be explored urgently through a fully funded public evaluation commissioned by the government. It also offers an insight into the subtleties of many of the issues at hand, which cannot easily be captured by headline figures. The qualitative data used here derives from interviews with ESOL learners – and those who are missing out on ESOL provision – and from three workshops held with stakeholders in the ESOL debate.

This chapter explores the impact of the current funding and delivery arrangements on the following key issues:

- meeting the needs of spouses
- meeting the needs of refugees and asylum seekers
- meeting the needs of those on low incomes

Meeting the needs of spouses

One key area of concern, raised previously by the REIA conducted on changes to ESOL entitlements,[60] is the impact of the changes on spouses. This concern was recognised by the government, and reflected in the creation of a £4.6 million hardship fund, in March 2007, to support vulnerable learners including spouses and low-paid workers.[61]

Tax credits are used as the barometer of whether someone is capable of paying for their own English course, or whether they should qualify for fee remission. Vitally, though, tax credits apply to *families* not individuals: tax credits are based on household income and circumstances.[62] For tax credits to work as a tool for determining means test thresholds, we need to be confident that household income equals personal spending power.

A key message from the workshops held with ESOL stakeholders – academics, college representatives, community groups and government agencies – is that many women in migrant communities neither work, nor have spending power of their own within the family unit. To deal with the first of these, the latest evidence on London shows that fathers, in general, are almost twice as likely to be in work than mothers (see table 1), with men as a whole 14 per cent more likely to be in work than women.

Table 1 **Worklessness by selected characteristics**

Characteristic	Rate of worklessness (London)	Rate of worklessness (rest of UK)
Working age	31	25
Men	24	21
Women	37	29
Parents (including lone parents)	39	27
Fathers	26	18
Mothers	49	34
Lone parents	55	41
White	25	24
Black or minority ethnic	41	38
Born in the UK	28	25
Born abroad	36	30

Source: *Labour Force Survey*, Spring 2006[63]

National data illustrates that this pattern is even clearer in migrant groups. Research for the Home Office has shown that employment rates for migrant men and women stand at 75 per cent and 56 per cent, respectively, compared with much higher – and less differentiated – figures of 84 per cent and 73 per cent for the UK-born population.[64] Migrant women are even less likely to be in work themselves than their UK-born counterparts. The Home Office found that the key factor making the difference between men and women seemed to be children: less than half of female migrants with children were found to be in work, compared with over three-quarters of men.[65]

This supports the findings of the independent Equalities Commission, which published a wide-ranging report last year:

The majority of inactive Pakistani and Bangladeshi women say they do not want to work because they are looking after the family and home. This was the reason given by almost two in three (63 per cent) of economically inactive Pakistani women and nearly three in four (72 per cent) of inactive Bangladeshi women. There is evidence that the reasons for Pakistani and Bangladeshi women's employment penalty arises from a belief that good motherhood involves staying at home and providing their own childcare.[66]

These trends – which of course do not apply to every migrant from the groups mentioned – were also broadly reflected in interviews for this project. It emerged frequently that many women now accessing ESOL provision had waited a number of years before registering for courses, because they felt a personal responsibility to bring up their children first.

This raises two vital issues for the ESOL strategies. First, it reveals that the goal of a demand-led system is insufficient. 'Demand' and 'need' are not the same thing and should not be treated as such. Simply meeting the needs of those who present themselves to register for courses will not help meet *need* – those people who are not 'demanding' a course, but would benefit from one. To achieve the social goals outlined at the beginning of the report, at an individual and social level, policy should focus on the needs of the disengaged and disenfranchised.

This points to the importance of effective outreach work that aims to *raise demand* by connecting with the hardest to reach – something that colleges are already involved in, but which should be supported and encouraged more systematically. Such work may well be difficult, time consuming and beyond either the interests or capacity of one provider. It may best be done in partnership with the third sector, which often has established networks with migrant communities and has built up levels of trust over time.

Further, those working in Sure Start and Extended Schools should be given guidance and training to help refer parents to English courses and to set up English courses in their own institutions with local colleges and other providers. *A range of initiatives to reach those most disengaged from learning need to be taken by local authorities and the LSC.* These might include funding community groups to do outreach work, and rewarding colleges and other providers already doing excellent outreach work beyond the call of duty.

There is, inevitably, the likelihood that some people will always choose not to learn English. The state can do little about this, nor should it have an interest in doing so. However, what can be expected is that the state does all it can to remove other barriers – such as awareness of opportunities, or confidence to take them up – to help people access classes that will improve the quality of their lives and of their interactions with others.

Second, large numbers of female migrants may be missing out on ESOL courses because they lack personal spending power. At the workshops held for this project, colleges report difficulties experienced by women unable to access either family money or even information about their family's financial position.

It cannot be assumed that an individual from a relatively wealthy family has their own spending power – or even that those from families nominally below the tax credit threshold will have access to financial information about their family's position. As with UK-born families of all backgrounds and cultures,[67] the glass ceiling may be in the home, rather than just the labour market, and the state should look to overcome, rather than reinforce that.

The issue of personal spending power versus family wealth illustrates that the state runs real risks and makes big assumptions if it channels entitlements for public services through the family unit. Increasing awareness of the needs of spouses – reflected in the government's hardship fund – is welcome. But the issue is not simply a problem of implementation; it is a fundamental feature of how the means test is constructed. The danger is that one policy is creating a problem, which a further policy – in the shape of the hardship fund – is then being asked to solve.

For the government and the mayor to achieve their goals of targeting support and funding at those who need it most, the state should treat people as individuals, rather than just as members of families. The clearest way of doing this would be for entitlements to fee remission to be structured around *non-employment* rather than unemployment. In other words, *fee remission should be available for all those without a job (ie their own spending power) rather than just those whose families are claiming tax credits.* This is an approach already used elsewhere, when benefit payments are made directly into individuals' bank accounts to ensure that they receive them.[68]

Extra funding to make these changes should come from across government (eg the Department for Communities and Local Government and the Home Office). As discussed earlier, learning English has wider benefits beyond the individual and beyond the labour market – and sources of funding should reflect this.

Ideally, the government would approach this in a coherent way, with funding channelled through a single budget, whether that would be the Skills for Life budget or a single cross-departmental budget for English language learning.

Meeting the needs of refugees and asylum seekers

Asylum seekers are an area of real concern. Again, following the REIA, changes were made to safeguard young asylum seekers and those still waiting for their cases to be processed after a period of six months. But the question, raised repeatedly in the workshops held for this project, remains on whether asylum seekers are the real cause of such rising demand – and whether the consequences of making them wait for six months before they are entitled to fee remission are acceptable.

First, the Home Office's evidence shows that 'annual asylum applications are at their lowest level since 1993'.[69]

Given that asylum claims have been falling steadily it seems contradictory to suggest that they are responsible for the marked rise in demand in recent years. Increased spending on ESOL in London and across the UK is not the result of rising asylum applications.

Second, the government and the mayor must ask themselves about the impact of leaving people without English language provision for six months. The impact on asylum seekers themselves is a major issue. As the Refugee Council has pointed out:

Asylum seekers are prevented from working and asylum support is only 70 per cent the rate of income support. They cannot be expected to pay for English courses... it is difficult to see how asylum seekers with poor or nonexistent English will get by in their area of dispersal, let alone feel part of local communities.[70]

Further, given some of the evidence outlined above about the importance of the English language as a force for greater integration and social cohesion, it seems risky on social as well as humanitarian grounds to wait for six months before offering fee remission. This is particularly the case for London, given that the standard Home Office assumption is that about 85 per cent of all UK asylum applicants live in the capital.[71] If further reason were needed, research by the National Research and Development Centre for Adult Literacy and Numeracy (NRDC) shows that new arrivals are more likely to make progress with learning English than those who may have already been in the country for six months before entering formal learning.[72]

A final factor to consider is that the majority of initial asylum decisions are now taken in just eight weeks.[73] In the light of this figure, it seems sensible that entitlements should be activated at this point for the unfortunate few who are still waiting for decisions on their cases. It would make most sense for the Home Office to bear at least some of the cost of this extension. This would both reflect the reasoning behind the change (issues of social cohesion) and would set a good incentive to continue to speed up the process of dealing with people's claims. However, as argued above, funding from any source needs to be channelled through one coordinated budget across London if provision is to meet need.

Meeting the needs of people on low incomes

A second area of concern, raised by ESOL stakeholders and in interviews with ESOL learners themselves, is the danger that those on the margins of the means test will be priced out of provision. In interviews with ESOL learners it became clear that many were opting for affordable courses rather than those which genuinely matched their needs. Others were enrolling in (free) literacy courses, rather than the English language courses designed to meet the needs of speakers of other languages. Those being asked to pay were often working in relatively low-paid jobs in the service industry, such as drivers or cleaners, and commonly expressed doubts about their ability to continue to pay fees of around £600 per course in the future.

Means testing will always be most difficult for those closest to thresholds and there will always be judgements for policy makers to make. However, it is vital that the threshold is set at the right level. This should be a key research question in future evaluations of the policy commissioned by government. The principle that those who will benefit – and can pay – should make some contribution also extends to employers. It is notable that in discussion of immigration, business emerges as a strong advocate of the economic value of migration. The reason is simple: migrant workers are good for business. Inward migration increases the supply of labour, bringing with it skills that businesses need.

Given this benefit, it seems fair that businesses should also make their contribution. Creating provision that meets the needs of businesses represents the carrot in this strategy, but the government has yet to identify any more assertive measures. One measure could be that *employers should be required to demonstrate how they are meeting health and safety requirements effectively if their employees are found to be without basic English.* Safety in the workplace extends beyond the ability to read, or memorise, health and safety procedures – it is about basic communication and if employers want to benefit from employing migrants, they should take measures to support their wellbeing. Similarly, companies seeking Investors in People or other quality kite marks and employing migrant workers should be expected to demonstrate a commitment to their employees learning English.

More broadly, the political issue of who benefits from migration, and where the costs lie, is an issue that political parties need to address. Even the biggest advocates for business are beginning to suggest that employers should be asked to make their fair contribution.[74]

5 Personalising provision

One of the most remarkable features of the population of ESOL learners (and potential learners) is its diversity – not just in terms of country of origin, or ethnic background, but also in educational background. This chapter argues that:

- Policy is not sufficiently flexible to meet the needs of English language learners with different motivations and end goals.
- Entitlements and delivery arrangements should be revised to address different starting points and different goals.

Meeting the needs of learners with different starting points

People access English courses from radically different starting points. Many learners are fully literate in their own language, while some have no, or very low, levels of literacy in their own language (see figure 4). Learning English for two different people, even if they have arrived from the same country, can be a completely different proposition: some are *learning to read and write through the English language*, while others may well be educated to very advanced levels and are learning a foreign language.[75]

A key challenge for policy and practice, therefore, is to produce learning opportunities tailored to the needs of the individual learners. Specifically, pace of learning is vital. Learning to read and write through the English language is likely to take considerably longer than simply learning a foreign language as a well-educated individual.

Figure 4 **Skill levels of London residents and recent migrants (%)**

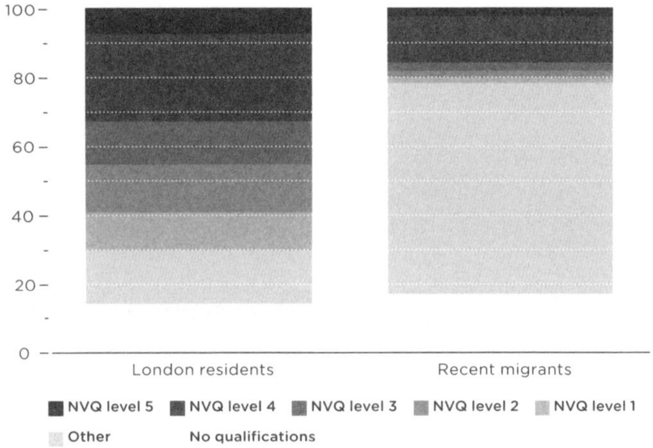

Source: *Labour Force Survey*, 2005
Note: Recent migrants are those who came to the UK in 2004 and currently live in London

As a result of this, those simply learning a foreign language are likely to progress far more quickly than those learning basic literacy *as well as* the English language. The question for policy, then, is how to encourage and support colleges and other providers to differentiate their offers according to the needs of their learners. To an extent this is already being driven independently by colleges and other providers that recognise the importance of placing people in the right courses, with other learners of similar starting points. The question is whether policy is helping or hindering this process and the problem is that entitlements are constructed around only two factors – economic status and levels of fluency in English. The result is that two other vital factors are not sufficiently taken into consideration – prior educational achievement and personal ambition.

The lack of attention paid to educational experience

and confidence, together with a lack of interest in learners' motivation, means that entitlements remain relatively insensitive to learners' needs. It is also wrong that funding establishes fixed expectations as to how long learners will take to progress. This risks creating a perverse incentive for providers to choose learners who are likely to succeed rather than those with the most educational need.

The solution to this problem could be to build all entitlements around a more holistic needs assessment of each individual than is currently available. This process would assess (a) people's level of English, (b) their literacy in their native language – a proxy for this would be to determine the number of years of education an individual has undertaken, (c) their eligibility for fee remission, and (d) their motives for learning and the mode of provision they would prefer.

One outcome of this approach might be to place people in pre-established funding bands, to reflect the length and intensity of courses that each individual would need.

The overall effect of the assessment would be to ensure that more money would go to those with low literacy levels in their own languages, low-level English and low/no income levels – reflecting the government's (and mayor's) own goals of personalising learning opportunities and targeting funding at those most in need.

The assessment process would also provide a good opportunity to offer non-English speakers advice and support to demonstrate their financial situation and ensure that they receive the correct entitlements. This is an issue that has already been raised as a barrier for non-English speakers[76] and has been recognised by government. The assessment process would be a natural way of addressing it.

The advice and guidance at this stage could also involve arrangements for work placements or other local 'immersion opportunities'. These mentoring, volunteering or shadowing opportunities would help people practise and apply what they will be learning in the classroom. This would reflect the importance of learning outside teaching hours[77] and would be a good staging post to help people play an active role in their communities.

The needs assessment would also help address some other issues specific to the different educational backgrounds of migrants. Both employers and governments find it difficult to identify the value of skills and qualifications that migrants bring with them, unless they were acquired in the British education system. The most recent estimate of the qualifications of the migrant workforce of London (see figure 4) shows half of all migrants with their skill levels classified as 'other'.[78] The lack of transferability of prior qualifications or work experience risks the skills of migrants being under-utilised – a problem for them and a waste for London. To help resolve this, *the needs assessment described above should also include investigation of skill levels and prior employment, with a view to helping people accredit existing skills where necessary or possible.* The government has indicated recently its desire to accredit the skills gained through informal training in the workplace; the principle would be the same here, helping migrants demonstrate their skills and put them to use in London.

Meeting the needs of learners with different end goals

A striking feature of the interviews conducted for this project was the range of end goals that learners had in mind when taking up an English language course. Some were learning to enhance their ability to communicate with others in their communities, some to give them the language skills to find employment, some to give them a platform to go on to further vocational learning, and some to support their children. Many learners felt that these goals were not sufficiently reflected in the standardised courses, which are the only ones available to them.

The question for policy is whether it is sufficiently capable, as things stand, of reflecting and supporting this huge breadth of goals. Policy makers have attempted to address this recently with the introduction of 'ESOL for Work' qualifications, which are designed to be 'shorter, simpler and more work focused, to better meet the needs of employers and those who need English for the workplace'.[79]

But the general direction of ESOL policy has been to rationalise provision, making it more homogenous. As the LSC's *Annual Statement of Priorities* puts it:

We will also be making other changes in Skills for Life and English for Speakers of Other Languages policy to meet ministerial requirements and improve the quality and relevance of provision... the number of publicly funded places on shorter courses that do not offer progression and contribute less directly to our targets will fall.[80]

The aim of the government to ensure that courses support progression is the right one. ESOL provision should help people improve over time until they reach the point where they no longer need to take part in courses. However, the danger with an overly prescriptive system is that it makes too many assumptions about what people are looking for and need from a course, inadvertently reducing the likelihood that learners' needs will be met.

There are some signs that this may be the case in practice. ESOL stakeholders are clear that entry-level courses, which are not themselves 'target-bearing', are proving much more difficult to fund, in comparison with courses leading to the higher qualifications that do contribute towards government targets. Evidence collected by the LSEB supports this, with a recent report stating:

National budgetary reallocations during 2007/8 have aimed to move resources into programmes such as Train to Gain from the Further Education Adult budget and to ensure that a greater share of residual adult funding is assigned to target-bearing provision (ie entry level 3 and above in the case of ESOL). One effect in London, however, has been an estimated projected fall in funding for entry level ESOL training of between £15 and £20 million, ie provision that disproportionately affects low income learners, often women from BAME [Black, Asian, Minority Ethnic] backgrounds.[81]

This echoes the forewarning in a document on the ESOL

evidence base, published by the LSC itself last year, which stated: 'In the case of ESOL, whole qualifications must be achieved rather than the parts that are most relevant to the learner or employer.'[82]

At the heart of this is the challenge of finding courses of learning – and course outcomes – which reflect the different reasons that people access ESOL courses. Some of the interviewees involved in our research, for example, were driven by the prospect of achieving a full qualification. They regarded it as a matter of pride and as a source of employability in the labour market. Others, however, had registered for courses with a very specific aim in mind – improving interviewing skills, for example.

The lesson is that ESOL courses culminating in full, traditional qualifications at the end of long courses are not always a good reflection of what individual learners or employers are looking for. An unintended consequence of this is that the learning and employment systems struggle to work together as effectively as they need to. While the skills system focuses principally on qualifications, the employment system is more focused on what it takes to help someone into work.

To meet people's needs more effectively – and to bridge the gap between the skills and the employment systems – *a credit-based framework for ESOL needs to be introduced as soon as possible. Under this system learners could access public funding for part of an overall qualification, rather than having to sign up for a whole course which they believe will not suit their needs.* This increased element of flexibility would help create more demand among individuals and employers – and the use of credits would help to ensure that courses were providing the important element of progression. It would enable learners to return to learning if and when they decide that they need it, while steadily building towards accreditation.

To protect entry-level courses, which are important stepping stones to progression, the effects of targets need to be reviewed. Culturally, targets need to be understood as approximate measures of progress, not outcomes in themselves, if policy is to avoid unintended consequences. More tangibly, the government should introduce a measure for entry-level courses if they are otherwise going to prove hard to fund.

A further important feature of the credit framework would be to introduce different forms of assessment for different courses. Credits – or at least a certain number of credits – should therefore be on offer without the need for a standardised, external assessment. Along with the proposed changes set out above, not all courses would end in a standardised assessment.

This would certainly not mean the end of standardised assessment – indeed it would be necessary to achieve a full qualification, but it would be a way of introducing a greater breadth of courses without the huge expense of having to externally accredit all learning, even when qualifications seem inappropriate.

This being the case what is needed is a system of measuring progress that is appropriate for progression within the education system and, just as importantly, provides satisfaction for the learner. This is most likely to come, in many cases, from a clear initial diagnosis and identification of goals at the outset, followed by provision and testing that reflects that. Changing the system would therefore not mean the end of qualifications, but it would lead to a wider range of options to meet a wider range of needs.

To reflect the goal of building provision around the needs of learners, the voice of learners needs to be brought to the heart of attempts to assure standards and high-quality provision. The aim should be to create feedback loops, through which the experience of learners would inform future policy and practice.

One way of achieving this would be *an online system of feedback, through which learners would reflect on their experience of a course on its completion.* Learners would be asked to reflect on the extent to which:

- they achieved what they wanted to out of the course
- the advice and guidance met their needs
- the course content met their needs
- the teaching met their needs

This feedback system would begin to create an aggregated picture of the learner experience in London, pointing to areas in need of improvement in the future. The quality of provision and the relevance of courses are important issues – and the best way to assess them is to ask learners themselves. The information provided through this system would inevitably be imperfect – measures would need to be taken to try to ensure that those dropping out of courses took part, for example – but it would provide an important resource for policy and practice in the future.

Finally, *to help encourage both more employers and individuals to invest in ESOL learning, funding arrangements should ensure that embedded courses (ie learning English and a vocational skill) would be eligible for fee remission.* People would be placed on these courses where and when this emerged as the right option from the personalised assessment. During interviews for this project, learners repeatedly expressed their frustration at not being able to draw down funding for embedded courses – the government should take the opportunity to address this, reflecting its own priorities to help Londoners and others across the UK gain new skills in adult life.

The risk, where the supply of learning opportunities reflects targets rather than what employers and individuals need, is that fewer people will benefit from courses. As with so many areas of policy, it is vital that targets are understood as approximate measures of success, rather than confused as outcomes in themselves.[83]

Conclusions and recommendations

Speaking earlier this year, the Minister for Further and Higher Education made the following pledge: 'I want to assure you, we will continue to monitor how these changes will impact our priority learners. We will continue to listen and work with all those with an interest in ESOL to ensure the best possible provision.'[84] This report has been written in that spirit. It has aimed to highlight the areas where policy is failing to achieve its stated goals of targeting help at those most in need – and helping as many people as possible to learn English as a result.

Our core argument is that while the principles on which policy has been established are sound, some radical changes may be needed to the way entitlements are put together and in the choices that are made available to learners. The overriding problem is that the rules for entitlements make too many assumptions – and risk excluding people, unintentionally, as a result – while the scope of how entitlements can be spent is too narrow to be based around the needs of each learner.

Many of the issues discussed in the report are being addressed through good practice in colleges and other providers. However, the issue is whether policy builds on these approaches and supports taking them to scale. The report and recommendations focus on the role policy can play in shaping the whole system. The recommendations are therefore directed at the government, the LSC, the LSEB and the Mayor of London.

Funding and entitlement

Recommendation 1: To ensure that spouses are not excluded unintentionally from provision, entitlements should treat people as individuals rather than as members of families – they should be structured around *non-employment* rather than unemployment.

In other words, fee remission should be available for all those without a job (ie their own spending power) rather than just for those whose families claim benefits.

This would solve an issue that the government already recognises and is trying to solve: the concern that spouses will miss out on provision through lack of personal spending power or access to their families' financial information.

Recommendation 2: To build flexibility, or personalisation, into the system, all entitlements should be established through a personal needs assessment, which would take account, among other factors, of prior levels of education.

Similarly, policy should avoid the assumption that all learners will progress at the same rate. Those with low levels of prior education are likely to be learning to read and write through the English language, rather than just learning a foreign language. For this reason they require longer, or more intensive, courses and therefore more financial support.

To build this flexibility, or personalisation, into the system, all entitlements should be established through a personal needs assessment.

Recommendation 3: During the needs assessment, people should be given advice about entitlements, assistance in finding the right course, guidance about how best to accredit existing skills, and direction towards immersion opportunities to supplement their learning.

These mentoring, volunteering or shadowing opportunities would help people practise and apply what they will be learning in the classroom.

Recommendation 4: On grounds of humanitarianism and social cohesion, funding arrangements for refugees and asylum seekers should also be reviewed.

Funding arrangements for asylum seekers should also be reviewed – due to falling asylum numbers, concerns about the wellbeing of asylum seekers themselves, and the issues of social cohesion. The majority of initial asylum decisions are now taken in just eight weeks; in the light of this, entitlements should be activated at this point for those who are still waiting for decisions on their cases. It would make most sense for the Home Office to bear at least some of the cost of this extension. This would both reflect the reasoning behind the change (issues of social cohesion) and create a good incentive for the Home Office to continue to speed up the process of dealing with people's claims.

Recommendation 5: To reflect social goals the government should aim not just to meet demand, but to meet *need* by connecting with the hardest to reach. This would involve outreach work, partnership with the third sector in signposting opportunities and guidance for other local public services.

This would mean finding ways to make people aware of opportunities and help offer encouragement for them to take them up. This could be done in a number of ways. Employers would be incentivised to offer basic English training through linking this to health and safety procedures and Investors in People accreditation. Other local service providers would be encouraged and trained, if necessary, to refer people on to courses. And discretionary money would be made available at a local level for outreach work.

Recommendation 6: These recommendations have cost implications. Where feasible, extra funding to make these changes should come from across government, reflecting the full range of goals associated with ESOL learning – personal empowerment, enhanced employability, improved social cohesion and greater intergenerational mobility. To ensure coherence, one department should take the lead on ESOL policy and funding control.

The recommendations above imply that there should be more investment from government to ensure that the goals of policy are met in practice. Importantly, these goals – personal, economic, social, intergenerational – map across a number of different government departments. Therefore, while it would be sensible for ESOL to be delivered through a single budget – nationally and for London – it also makes sense to regard this as more than simply a 'skills' issue. Funding should therefore come from a range of sources, including the Department for Innovation, Universities and Skills; the Home Office; and Communities and Local Government, and cross-cutting money set aside to promote community cohesion in London.

Delivery

Recommendation 7: To create options for learning that meet people's specific needs, the government should establish a credit framework for ESOL courses, to provide both the option of shorter courses and a platform for progression.

Just as funding arrangements should avoid making too many assumptions about people's needs and ability to pay without some genuine interactions with learners themselves, delivery arrangements should avoid assumptions about why people are learning and what they should be learning from their courses.

In particular, there needs to be much greater flexibility about the length of courses. There needs to be the option of short courses, which still provide progression, along the lines of the proposed qualifications credit framework, which will enable people to build up credits towards a qualification, should that be their desired end goal.

Recommendation 8: To add flexibility to the system, national policy should experiment with different forms of assessment – such as practitioner assessment for a certain number of credits of learning within each qualification – and ensure that embedded ESOL courses are eligible for fee remission.

To achieve a qualification that would be recognised across London and the rest of the country, it would be important that learners passed a standardised, national assessment. However, for shorter courses it would be a waste of resources to have to externally accredit every element of learning, particularly short courses of learning, designed for a specific need.

Credits – or at least a certain number of credits – should therefore be on offer without the need for a standardised, external assessment. This would also help bridge the gap between the demand for job-specific training and the LSC's ability to fund courses. Colleges' assessment procedures, should they offer these courses, would be part of any external inspection.

Embedded courses (ie learning English *and* a vocational skill) would also be fundable with public money. People would be placed on these courses where and when this emerged as the right option from the personalised assessment.

Recommendation 9: To bring the learner's voice to the heart of the system there should be a national online system of feedback, through which learners would reflect on their experience of a course on its completion.

Personalised provision is predicated on gaining information from service users about their needs, ambitions and experiences. One way of achieving this would be to collect information on how learners at different institutions experience different courses. This would provide an invaluable source of information for learners, practioners and policy makers to make better decisions about future provision.

Recommendation 10: To protect entry-level courses, which are important stepping stones to progression, the effects of targets need to be reviewed. Targets need to be understood as approximate measures of progress, not outcomes in themselves, if policy is to avoid unintended consequences. More tangibly, the government should introduce a measure for entry-level courses if they are going to prove hard to fund otherwise.

Government has a legitimate role in ensuring that taxpayers' money is well spent. Part of fulfilling this inevitably means measuring progress against an agreed set of goals. What is important, though, is that targets do not skew provision away from meeting the needs of learners – the primary goal of policy. This requires understanding targets for what they are: rough markers of progress, not ends in themselves.

Treating them as if they were outcomes and using them to drive change too aggressively risks adverse outcomes. This is a cultural issue to some extent, but the unintended effects of targets might also be mitigated against through the introduction of targets for entry-level courses. It is not the intention of policy that funding for entry-level courses should be cut, so this could be one way of ensuring that they are protected.

Future policy and strategy

Recommendation 11: To ensure openness and transparency in future policy, the Mayor of London and the government should set out a clear statement of goals for English language policy in London.

One of the most important things that both the government and the mayor can do is to spell out a clear statement of goals for English language policy. The absence of this, at the time of writing, makes it very difficult to put together coherent policy across government, fund provision and measure progress over time.

Recommendation 12: To support effective policy and proper accountability, the government should commit to formal evaluations of English language policy against its stated objectives.

Once a clear statement of objectives has been established, the mayor and the government should commit to formal evaluations of English language policy against these goals. The changes already introduced by the government need to be tested over time to inform the future direction of policy. These evaluations should be both comprehensive and public.

Taken together these proposals add up to a significant shift in the way ESOL is funded and delivered. They require a new approach and mindset – more coordination across government, more flexibility for entitlements to match people's circumstances and more scope for courses of learning to be shaped around the needs of individual learners rather than national targets. However, we believe the potential pay-off to London would be significant, with greater numbers accessing courses that suit them and reaping the benefits for themselves and for London as a whole. London is a global city. For it to be as unified, fair and prosperous as it can be its people need access to a common language.

Afterword

The evidence and arguments put forward in this report suggest some wider policy lessons. We summarise them briefly below.

Targets need to be understood as approximate measures of progress, not outcomes in themselves, if policy is to avoid unintended consequences

The paradox for govenments is that while they aim to improve outcomes for people (for example better life chances, better health) they cannot deliver these achievements on their own. To solve this problem, policy makers measure outputs (qualifications, hospital waiting times) as a way of benchmarking the value added by services.

However, the danger with targets based on outputs is that they become conflated with outcomes when the two are not the same thing. For example, policies focus solely on full qualifications to achieve central targets, when what some people really need are short courses of learning – perhaps credits, which do not add up to full qualifications. The danger is that too narrow a focus on outputs gets in the way of outcomes.

This is not to argue that targets are never useful. Rather it implies that targets need to be used as one measure of policy rather than to drive change from the centre to the exclusion of all else. If targets impose unhelpful restrictions on systems then they become unhelpful.

Policy needs to be sensitive in how it interacts with families if it is to reach and empower the most vulnerable

In some areas of policy, family life is difficult to ignore. For example, children's services seek to see the child 'in context': problems may be solved through working with peers, teachers or parents – not just children in isolation. However, the state needs to be careful about viewing people through the prism of family relationships. The danger is that policy assumes that family structures are democratic, when they may not be, and reinforces rather than helps alleviate that problem. This is not an issue about any one culture, but a broader point about how the state 'sees' and interacts with people that requires consideration.

Personalised services are likely to require differentiated entitlements if they are to deliver on equality

The simple idea at the heart of personalised services is that people have different needs and starting points. The insight that follows is that for a service to be both effective and fair it must recognise those different needs and respond in ways that meet them. The same service will not work for everyone; fairness depends on differentiation.

This is a principle that can, in some circumstances, be applied in practice without changes to policy. Teachers can recognise different learning styles, interests and aptitudes and tailor learning opportunities for individual pupils, for example. Yet for personalisation to be taken to its logical conclusion, meeting the needs of some service users may require more resources to achieve than meeting those of others.

ESOL learning is the example in this report – teaching people to read *and* learn English is likely to require more teaching hours and other resources than teaching someone else a foreign language. In this case, policy – not just practice – has to adapt if personalisation is going to become a reality. Service providers must be flexible, but there must be resources that both support and encourage that flexibility. Without this, there will always be limitations on the extent to which a service can be moulded to the needs of an individual.

Segmentation is not the same as personalisation; this means entitlement *frameworks* can be constructed at the centre but that, ultimately, decisions will need to be taken outside Westminster through interactions with people themselves

Differentiated entitlements are, of course, already a feature of the welfare state. The problem is that the mechanism for achieving this is often segmentation of people according to 'client groups'. One good example of this is welfare provision: over the last ten years there has been a New Deal for Young People, a New Deal 25 plus, a New Deal 50 plus, a New Deal for Lone Parents, a New Deal for Disabled People, a New Deal for Partners and even a New Deal for Musicians.

This helps build in some recognition that people have different needs that will require different responses, but the danger is that this approach starts with a category rather than someone's personal needs and circumstances. Again, this makes sense for policy makers looking for simplicity and predictability in service delivery, but cramps room for genuine flexibility and personalisation.

The lesson here is that policy makers can set frameworks from central government without overriding decision making and damaging flexibility:

- *Principles* can be established – eg to focus the most resources on those most in need.
- *Guidelines* can be provided – eg to be aware that those without basic literacy and numeracy may require extra support in learning English.
- *Accountability* can recognise those guidelines, but be focused broadly on principles – eg to expect practice broadly to follow guidance, but to recognise that there will be instances in which the guidelines are inappropriate and where service providers should be able to explain their departure from them.
- *Funding* can be differentiated, without predetermining how much any individual might receive – eg the use of a needs assessment to truly understand a person's needs, which services they require and how those services might best be configured.

Demand-led and market-led are not the same thing; the state needs to deliver where the market mechanism (even when publicly funded) would not

In the language of public management, 'demand-led' is often equated with 'market-led'. In truth, the two terms overlap but are not the same thing. Markets respond where there is *sufficient* demand for something, rather than simply where there is *any* demand for it. In this sense they are often based on 'big hits', rather than niche needs that are very difficult to cater for.

For example, Blockbuster doesn't carry all the DVDs that people want to watch, it carries the most popular titles. There is a 'long-tail' of films that will never make it into the video store, but for which there is still *some* demand.[85] The point here is that public services are different from private markets: they have goals embedded in them like equality and fairness, which operators in the private market are not obliged to consider. Video shops are there to meet demand, not need.

Truly demand-led systems of public services, therefore, have to find ways of meeting the needs of all service users – and potential service users. Funding that follows the pupil is one way of working towards this, but requires the state to ensure that there isn't a 'market failure' for the most vulnerable. It can do this through contracts which specify 'full coverage' for services, as with some utilities, or it can use funding mechanisms to ensure all service users, whatever their personal circumstances, are attractive to service providers. But the important point is that in any 'demand-led' system, policy needs to ensure that those whose needs are greatest will not lose out further.

Demand-led and needs-led are not the same thing; the goal of publicly funded services should be to meet need, not just respond to demand

Linked to this last point is the insight that 'demand-led' and 'needs-led' are not the same thing. This may appear to be a semantic point but there is a genuine danger that services meet the needs only of those who turn up to register, 'demanding' a service. In many cases it is the most vulnerable who never access services in the first place, let alone losing out to those whose needs are easier to meet once they are in contact with the welfare state. The danger is that services configure around demand when there are those missing out who are in need (unarticulated demand).

The point here is that services need to be encouraged, supported and rewarded for creating demand through outreach work by engaging the disadvantaged. Again, the policy tools for this are various – referral systems from other services, funding mechanisms that encourage outreach work and greater partnership with the third sector. The key point is that the flexibility of a demand-led system needs to be supplemented with the right policies that ensure that all needs are met, rather than just those of the most engaged and articulate.

Notes

1 Throughout the report, the term ESOL is used as shorthand for all English language provision and support for adult speakers of other languages.

2 *The London Skills for Life Strategy.*

3 Rammell, 'ESOL funding is in safe hands', *TES*.

4 'London and New York emerge as clear leaders in new ranking of global financial centres', news release; and *Hansard*, 28 Nov 2006, Column 1016, see www.publications.parliament.uk/pa/cm200607/cmhansrd/cm061128/debtext/61128-0011.htm (accessed 12 Mar 2008).

5 *Country of Birth and Labour Market Outcomes in London.*

6 McRae, 'The resurgent city', speech.

7 JH Consulting, *Developing a Three Year Strategic Action Plan for Skills for Life in London.*

8 *The London Story.*

9 Kyambi, *Beyond Black and White.*

10 *London Skills for Life Strategy.*

11 Ibid.

12 Bentley, *It's Democracy Stupid.*

13 Miliband, 'The fight against fate', speech; Cameron, 'It's time to share power with the people', speech; 'Liberal intent', *Guardian*.

14 *London Economic Development Snapshot January 2007*.

15 *London Skills for Life Strategy*.

16 *Country of Birth and Labour Market Outcomes in London*.

17 Ibid.

18 *London Strategic Analysis 2007/08*.

19 Ipsos MORI, 'Annual London Survey 2006'.

20 Cantle (chair), *Community Cohesion*.

21 *Fairness and Freedom*.

22 Putnam, 'E Pluribus Unum', lecture.

23 *'What Works' in Community Cohesion*.

24 Commission on Integration and Cohesion, *Our Shared Future*.

25 Blanden and Machin, *Recent Changes in Intergenerational Mobility in the UK*.

26 *Intergenerational Mobility in Europe and North America*.

27 Feinstein, 'Inequality in the early cognitive development of British children in the 1970 cohort', *Economica*.

28 For a review of the evidence see *Every Parent Matters*.

29 Desforges, *The Impact of Parental Involvement, Parental Support and Family Education on Pupil Achievements and Adjustment*.

30 *Fairness and Freedom.*

31 *Country of Birth and Labour Market Outcomes in London.*
32 *Fairness and Freedom.*

33 *Prosperity for All in a Global Economy.*

34 Office for National Statistics, *Labour Force Survey*, 2006.

35 Rammell, 'ESOL funding is in safe hands', *TES*.

36 *London Skills for Life Strategy.*

37 Grover (chair), *More than a Language.*

38 *Annual Statement of Priorities 2006.*

39 Ibid.

40 Ibid.

41 Ford, 'Concessions granted on English for asylum seekers', *Guardian*.

42 *New English Language Qualifications for Migrant Workers and Employers.*

43 *Annual Statement of Priorities 2006.*

44 Ibid.

45 Ford, 'Concessions granted on English for asylum seekers', *Guardian*.

46 'Bill Rammell publishes race impact assessment and announces new measures', press notice.

47 Quoted in Ford, 'Concessions granted on English for asylum seekers', *Guardian*.

48 *ESOL: Urgent funding package 2007/08.*

49 Denham, Foreword to *Focusing English for Speakers of Other Languages (ESOL) on Community Cohesion*.

50 Grover (chair), *More than a Language*.

51 Kline, 'The unkindest cut', *Guardian*.

52 *Annual Statement of Priorities 2006.*

53 *London Story.*

54 *Prosperity for All in a Global Economy.*

55 Office for National Statistics, *Labour Force Survey*, 2006.

56 *Country of Birth and Labour Market Outcomes in London*.

57 Ibid.

58 Ibid.

59 *Annual Statement of Priorities 2006.*

60 *Race Equality Impact Assessment on Proposed Changes to the Funding Arrangements of English for Speakers of Other Languages and Asylum Seeker Eligibility for Learning and Skills Council Further Education Funding.*

61 'Bill Rammell publishes race impact assessment and announces new measures', press notice.

62 See www.direct.gov.uk/en/MoneyTaxAndBenefits/TaxCreditsandChildBenefit/TaxCredits/DG_4015478 (accessed 12 Mar 2008).

63 *London Story.*

64 *Skills Audit of Refugees.*
65 Ibid.

66 *Fairness and Freedom.*

67 Green and Parker, *The Other Glass Ceiling.*

68 See www.dwp.gov.uk/directpayment/ (accessed 12 Mar 2008).

69 'Minister pledges fast but fair asylum system', press notice.

70 *ESOL and Further Education Funding Changes 2007/08 announced by the Learning and Skills Council.*

71 *Refugees and Asylum Seekers in London.*

72 Baynham et al, *Effective Teaching and Learning ESOL.*

73 *ESOL and Further Education Funding Changes 2007/08 announced by the Learning and Skills Council.*

74 Stelzer, 'Employers should bear the cost of immigration', *Daily Telegraph.*

75 *London Story.*

76 Kline, 'The unkindest cut', *Guardian.*

77 National Research and Development Centre for Adult Literacy and Numeracy, *Basic Skills and Social Inclusion.*

78 *London Story.*

79 *Hansard*, 1 Feb 2007, Column 486W, see www.publications.parliament.uk/pa/cm200607/cmhansrd/cm070201/text/70201w0016.htm (accessed 12 Mar 2008).

80 *Annual Statement of Priorities 2006.*

81 *London Story.*

82 *London Strategic Action Plan for Skills for Life in London.*

83 Chapman, *System Failure.*

84 Rammell, speech.

85 Anderson, 'The long tail', *Wired.*

References

Anderson, C, 'The long tail', *Wired Magazine* 12.20, Oct 2004.

Annual Statement of Priorities 2006 (London: Learning and Skills Council, 2006).

Baynham, M et al, *Effective Teaching and Learning ESOL* (London: National Research and Development Centre for Adult Literacy and Numeracy, 2007).

Bentley, T, *It's Democracy Stupid: An agenda for self-government* (London: Demos, 2001).

'Bill Rammell publishes race impact assessment and announces new measures', press notice, DfES, 26 Mar 2007.

Blanden, J and Machin, S, *Recent Changes in Intergenerational Mobility in the UK* (London: Sutton Trust, 2007).

Cameron, D, 'It's time to share power with the people', speech at the Power Inquiry conference, 6 May 2006.

Cantle, T (chair), *Community Cohesion: A report of the independent review team* (London: Home Office, 2001).

Chapman, J, *System Failure: Why governments must learn to think differently* (London: Demos, 2002).

Commission on Integration and Cohesion, *Our Shared Future: Report of the Commission on Integration and Cohesion* (Wetherby: Communities and Local Government Publications, 2007).

Country of Birth and Labour Market Outcomes in London: An analysis of Labour Force Survey and Census data (London: Greater London Authority, Data Management and Analysis Group Briefing, 2005).

Denham, J, Foreword to *Focusing English for Speakers of Other Languages (ESOL) on Community Cohesion* (London: HM Government, 2008).

Desforges, C, *The Impact of Parental Involvement, Parental Support and Family Education on Pupil Achievements and Adjustment: A literature review* (London: DfES, 2003).

ESOL and Further Education Funding Changes 2007/08 announced by the Learning and Skills Council, briefing document (London: Refugee Council, 2007).

ESOL: Urgent funding package 2007/08 (London: London Development Agency, 2006).

Every Parent Matters (London: Department for Education and Skills, 2006).

Fairness and Freedom: The final report of the Equalities Review (London: Cabinet Office, 2007).

Feinstein, L, 'Inequality in the early cognitive development of British children in the 1970 cohort', *Economica* 70, no 1 (Feb 2003).

Ford, L, 'Concessions granted on English for asylum seekers', *Guardian*, 7 Mar 2007.

Green, H and Parker, S, *The Other Glass Ceiling: The domestic politics of parenting* (London: Demos, 2006).

Grover, D (chair), *More than a Language: Final report of the NIACE Committee of Inquiry on English for Speakers of Other Languages (ESOL)* (Leicester: National Institute of Adult Continuing Education, 2006).

Hansard, see www.publications.parliament.uk/pa/pahansard.htm (accessed 12 Mar 2008).

Intergenerational Mobility in Europe and North America (London: London School of Economics, 2005).

Ipsos MORI, 'Annual London Survey 2006: Final topline results', 30 Jan 2007, see www.london.gov.uk/mayor/annual_survey/2006/als-2006-toplines.pdf (accessed 12 Mar 2008).

JH Consulting, *Developing a Three Year Strategic Action Plan for Skills for Life in London: Summary of evidence and recommendations for ESOL* (London: Learning and Skills Council, 2005).

Kline, R, 'The unkindest cut', *Guardian*, 7 Jan 2007.

Kyambi, S, *Beyond Black and White: Mapping new immigrant communities* (London: Institute for Public Policy Research, 2005).

'Liberal intent', *Guardian*, 21 Oct 2007.

'London and New York emerge as clear leaders in new ranking of global financial centres', news release, City of London, 7 Nov 2005, see www.cityoflondon.gov.uk/Corporation/media_centre/files2006/London+and+New+York+global+financial+leaders.htm (accessed 12 Mar 2008).

London Economic Development Snapshot January 2007 (London: London Development Agency, 2007).

The London Skills for Life Strategy (London: London Development Agency, 2006).

The London Story: Globalisation, employment and skills (London: London Skills and Employment Board, 2007).

London Strategic Action Plan for Skills for Life in London: Summary of evidence for literacy, numeracy and key skills (London: LSC, 2006).

The London Strategic Analysis 2007/08 (London: Learning and Skills Council, 2007).

McRae, H, 'The resurgent city', speech to Leverhulme International Symposium (2004), www.lse.ac.uk/collections/resurgentCity/Papers/hamishmcrae.pdf (accessed 12 Mar 2008).

Miliband, D, 'The fight against fate', speech to the Fabian Society, 30 Mar 2006.

'Minister pledges fast but fair asylum system: new asylum teams for West London and the South East', press notice, Home Office, 7 Feb 2007.

National Research and Development Centre for Adult Literacy and Numeracy, *Basic Skills and Social Inclusion*, briefing (London: NRDC, 2005).

New English Language Qualifications for Migrant Workers and Employers (London: DfES, 2007).

Office for National Statistics, *Labour Force Survey*, 2006 (London: ONS, 2006).

Prosperity for All in a Global Economy: World class skills, final report of the Leitch Review of Skills (London: HM Treasury, 2006).

Putnam, R, 'E Pluribus Unum: Diversity and community in the twenty-first century', Johan Skytte Prize Lecture, 2006.

Race Equality Impact Assessment on Proposed Changes to the Funding Arrangements of English for Speakers of Other Languages and Asylum Seeker Eligibility for Learning and Skills Council Further Education Funding – Report and Emerging Proposals (London: DfES, 2007).

Rammell, B, 'ESOL funding is in safe hands', *Times Education Supplement*, 25 May 2007.

Rammell, B, speech, NIACE conference on ESOL, Mar 2007.

Refugees and Asylum Seekers in London: A GLA perspective (London: Greater London Authority, 2001).

Skills Audit of Refugees (London: Home Office, 2004).

Stelzer, I, 'Employers should bear the cost of immigration', *Daily Telegraph*, 15 Aug 2007.

'What Works' in Community Cohesion (London: HM Government, 2007).

Demos – Licence to Publish

The work (as defined below) is provided under the terms of this licence ('licence'). The work is protected by copyright and/or other applicable law. Any use of the work other than as authorized under this licence is prohibited. By exercising any rights to the work provided here, you accept and agree to be bound by the terms of this licence. Demos grants you the rights contained here in consideration of your acceptance of such terms and conditions.

1 Definitions

A **'Collective Work'** means a work, such as a periodical issue, anthology or encyclopedia, in which the Work in its entirety in unmodified form, along with a number of other contributions, constituting separate and independent works in themselves, are assembled into a collective whole. A work that constitutes a Collective Work will not be considered a Derivative Work (as defined below) for the purposes of this Licence.

B **'Derivative Work'** means a work based upon the Work or upon the Work and other pre-existing works, such as a musical arrangement, dramatization, fictionalization, motion picture version, sound recording, art reproduction, abridgment, condensation, or any other form in which the Work may be recast, transformed, or adapted, except that a work that constitutes a Collective Work or a translation from English into another language will not be considered a Derivative Work for the purpose of this Licence.

C **'Licensor'** means the individual or entity that offers the Work under the terms of this Licence.

D **'Original Author'** means the individual or entity who created the Work.

E **'Work'** means the copyrightable work of authorship offered under the terms of this Licence.

F **'You'** means an individual or entity exercising rights under this Licence who has not previously violated the terms of this Licence with respect to the Work,or who has received express permission from Demos to exercise rights under this Licence despite a previous violation.

2 Fair Use Rights

Nothing in this licence is intended to reduce, limit, or restrict any rights arising from fair use, first sale or other limitations on the exclusive rights of the copyright owner under copyright law or other applicable laws.

3 Licence Grant

Subject to the terms and conditions of this Licence, Licensor hereby grants You a worldwide, royalty-free, non-exclusive,perpetual (for the duration of the applicable copyright) licence to exercise the rights in the Work as stated below:

A to reproduce the Work, to incorporate the Work into one or more Collective Works, and to reproduce the Work as incorporated in the Collective Works;

B to distribute copies or phonorecords of, display publicly,perform publicly, and perform publicly by means of a digital audio transmission the Work including as incorporated in Collective Works; The above rights may be exercised in all media and formats whether now known or hereafter devised.The above rights include the right to make such modifications as are technically necessary to exercise the rights in other media and formats. All rights not expressly granted by Licensor are hereby reserved.

4 Restrictions

The licence granted in Section 3 above is expressly made subject to and limited by the following restrictions:

A You may distribute,publicly display, publicly perform, or publicly digitally perform the Work only under the terms of this Licence, and You must include a copy of, or the Uniform Resource Identifier for, this Licence with every copy or phonorecord of the Work You distribute, publicly display,publicly perform, or publicly digitally perform.You may not offer or impose any terms on the Work that alter or restrict the terms of this Licence or the recipients' exercise of the rights granted hereunder.You may not sublicence the Work.You must keep intact all notices that refer to this Licence and to the disclaimer of warranties. You may not distribute, publicly display, publicly perform, or publicly digitally perform the Work with any technological measures that control access or use of the Work in a manner inconsistent with the terms of this Licence Agreement.The above applies to the Work as incorporated in a Collective Work, but this does not require the Collective Work apart from the Work itself to be made subject to the terms of this Licence. If You create a Collective Work, upon notice from any Licencor You must, to the extent practicable, remove from the Collective Work any reference to such Licensor or the Original Author, as requested.

B You may not exercise any of the rights granted to You in Section 3 above in any manner that is primarily intended for or directed toward commercial advantage or private monetary compensation.The exchange of the Work for other copyrighted works by means of digital filesharing or otherwise shall not be considered to be intended for or directed toward commercial advantage or private monetary compensation, provided there is no payment of any monetary compensation in connection with the exchange of copyrighted works.

C If you distribute, publicly display, publicly perform, or publicly digitally perform the Work or any Collective Works,You must keep intact all copyright notices for the Work and give the Original Author credit reasonable to the medium or means You are utilizing by conveying the name (or pseudonym if applicable) of the Original Author if supplied; the title of the Work if supplied. Such credit may be implemented in any reasonable manner; provided, however, that in the case of a Collective Work, at a minimum such credit will appear where any other comparable authorship credit appears and in a manner at least as prominent as such other comparable authorship credit.

5 Representations, Warranties and Disclaimer

A By offering the Work for public release under this Licence, Licensor represents and warrants that, to the best of Licensor's knowledge after reasonable inquiry:

i Licensor has secured all rights in the Work necessary to grant the licence rights hereunder and to permit the lawful exercise of the rights granted hereunder without You having any obligation to pay any royalties, compulsory licence fees, residuals or any other payments;

ii The Work does not infringe the copyright, trademark, publicity rights, common law rights or any other right of any third party or constitute defamation, invasion of privacy or other tortious injury to any third party.

B except as expressly stated in this licence or otherwise agreed in writing or required by applicable law,the work is licenced on an 'as is'basis,without warranties of any kind, either express or implied including,without limitation,any warranties regarding the contents or accuracy of the work.

6 Limitation on Liability

Except to the extent required by applicable law, and except for damages arising from liability to a third party resulting from breach of the warranties in section 5, in no event will licensor be liable to you on any legal theory for any special, incidental,consequential, punitive or exemplary damages arising out of this licence or the use of the work, even if licensor has been advised of the possibility of such damages.

7 Termination

A This Licence and the rights granted hereunder will terminate automatically upon any breach by You of the terms of this Licence. Individuals or entities who have received Collective Works from You under this Licence,however, will not have their licences terminated provided such individuals or entities remain in full compliance with those licences. Sections 1, 2, 5, 6, 7, and 8 will survive any termination of this Licence.

B Subject to the above terms and conditions, the licence granted here is perpetual (for the duration of the applicable copyright in the Work). Notwithstanding the above, Licensor reserves the right to release the Work under different licence terms or to stop distributing the Work at any time; provided, however that any such election will not serve to withdraw this Licence (or any other licence that has been, or is required to be, granted under the terms of this Licence), and this Licence will continue in full force and effect unless terminated as stated above.

8 Miscellaneous

A Each time You distribute or publicly digitally perform the Work or a Collective Work, Demos offers to the recipient a licence to the Work on the same terms and conditions as the licence granted to You under this Licence.

B If any provision of this Licence is invalid or unenforceable under applicable law, it shall not affect the validity or enforceability of the remainder of the terms of this Licence, and without further action by the parties to this agreement, such provision shall be reformed to the minimum extent necessary to make such provision valid and enforceable.

C No term or provision of this Licence shall be deemed waived and no breach consented to unless such waiver or consent shall be in writing and signed by the party to be charged with such waiver or consent.

D This Licence constitutes the entire agreement between the parties with respect to the Work licensed here.There are no understandings, agreements or representations with respect to the Work not specified here. Licensor shall not be bound by any additional provisions that may appear in any communication from You.This Licence may not be modified without the mutual written agreement of Demos and You.